The Magic of New Zealand

The Magic
of
New of Zealand

Published in 2000 by
New Holland Kowhai
An imprint of New Holland Publishers (NZ) Ltd
Auckland • Sydney • London • Cape Town

218 Lake Road
Northcote, Auckland
New Zealand

14 Aquatic Drive
Frenchs Forest, NSW 2086
Australia

86-88 Edgware Road
London W2 2EA
United Kingdom

80 McKenzie Street
Cape Town 8001
South Africa

www.newhollandpublishers.com

First published in 1998 by New Holland Publishers (NZ) Ltd

Copyright © 1998 New Holland Publishers (NZ) Ltd
Copyright © 1998 in text: Graeme Lay
Copyright © 1998 in photographs: Holger Leue,
with the exception of David Wall: pages 8, 25, 26 and 35;
Visual Impact Pictures: pages 22–23; Gray Clapham: pages 50–51

ISBN 1 877246 37 9

5 7 9 10 8 6 4

Designer: Janice Evans
Cover design: Sally Hollis-McLeod
Editor: Simon Pooley
Cartographer: Elaine Fick
Publishing Manager: Mariëlle Renssen
Reproduction by Hirt & Carter Cape (Pty) Ltd
Printed and bound by Times Offset (M) Sdn Bhd

Contents

PAGE ONE *Pastures, grazing sheep and a copse of hardy cabbage trees (Cordyline australis) near Farewell Spit, the South Island's northern extremity.*

PAGES TWO AND THREE *Beachside settlement at remote Waihau Bay, East Coast, North Island.*

PAGES FOUR AND FIVE *Afternoon sailing regatta on Lake Taupo, which occupies a vast crater created by a volcanic eruption in the central North Island.*

ABOVE *Brothers-in-arms. Tame Iti and Paora Rangiaho, Ruatahuna, Urewera region.*

PAGES EIGHT AND NINE *Te Pihopatanga o Aotearoa or Christ Church of New Zealand, Raukokore, East Coast, North Island. Unfortunately the magnificent Norfolk pines no longer stand sentinel over this elegant country church. Diseased, they were felled in August 2001.*

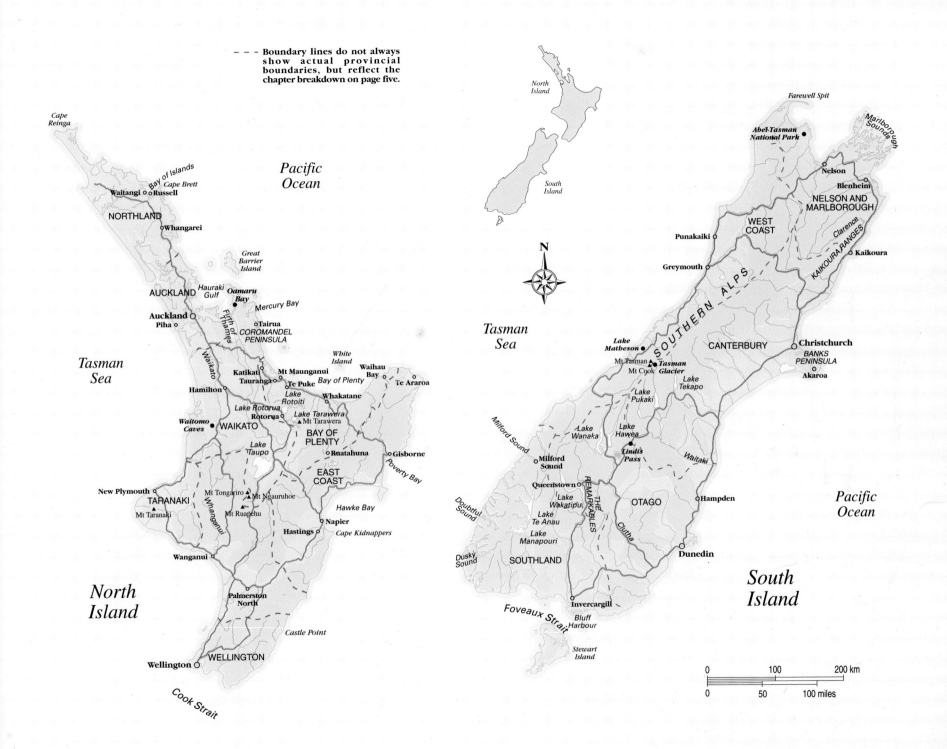

Boundary lines do not always show actual provincial boundaries, but reflect the chapter breakdown on page five.

North Island

Cape Reinga

Pacific Ocean

Bay of Islands
Cape Brett
Waitangi Russell
NORTHLAND
Whangarei

Great Barrier Island

Tasman Sea

AUCKLAND
Hauraki Gulf *Oamaru Bay*
Mercury Bay
Auckland
Piha Tairua
Firth of Thames COROMANDEL PENINSULA

White Island
Waihau Bay
Katikati Mt Maunganui Te Araroa
Tauranga Te Puke Bay of Plenty
Hamilton Lake Rotoiti
Whakatane
Lake Rotorua
Waitomo Caves Rotorua
WAIKATO Lake Tarawera
▲ Mt Tarawera
BAY OF PLENTY
Lake Taupo Ruatahuna Gisborne
EAST COAST Poverty Bay

New Plymouth Mt Tongariro
TARANAKI ▲ Mt Ngauruhoe
▲ Mt Taranaki Whanganui ▲ Mt Ruapehu
Hawke Bay
Napier
Hastings Cape Kidnappers

Wanganui

North Island

Palmerston North

Castle Point

Wellington WELLINGTON

Cook Strait

South Island

North Island
South Island

N

Farewell Spit

Abel-Tasman National Park
Nelson
Blenheim
NELSON AND MARLBOROUGH
WEST COAST
Marlborough Sounds
Punakaiki Clarence KAIKOURA RANGES Kaikoura
Greymouth
SOUTHERN ALPS

Tasman Sea

Lake Matheson
Mt Tasman CANTERBURY Christchurch
Mt Cook *Tasman Glacier* BANKS PENINSULA
Lake Tekapo Akaroa
Lake Pukaki

Milford Sound
Lake Wanaka *Lindis Pass*
Milford Sound Lake Hawea Waitaki
Queenstown Lake Wakatipu
Doubtful Sound THE REMARKABLES OTAGO Hampden
Lake Te Anau Clutha
Lake Manapouri
Dusky Sound SOUTHLAND

Pacific Ocean

Invercargill Dunedin
Bluff Harbour
Foveaux Strait
Stewart Island

South Island

0   100   200 km
0   50   100 miles

Introduction

*F*irstly, they notice the light. Strong and clear, it is the same clarity that delighted the Victorian painters who first depicted New Zealand's landscapes. After the light, visitors are struck by the emptiness of the land. Hills, plains and coasts are seemingly devoid of human habitation. Clear light and apparent emptiness: this is what newcomers first notice, this is what delights them.

New Zealand is two large islands and many small ones. It is a long land, extending through 15° of latitude from a sub-tropical north to a sub-Antarctic south. It is a country only a little smaller than Italy or Britain, yet its population is a fraction of theirs. There are just over 4 million New Zealanders. That is half the population of London, living in a country about the same size as Italy, which has 58 million people.

And within New Zealand's 265,150 sq. km (102,350 sq. miles) there is a breathtaking variety of landscapes. In the extreme south, there are fiords as grand as those of Norway; in the central South Island an alpine spine as serrated and snow-covered as the Andes; in the central North Island, a plateau as volcanically active as Iceland. There are the intricate waterways of the Marlborough Sounds, the horizon-wide plains of Canterbury, the sand dunes of Northland, the glacial lakes of central Otago, the lush forests of Westland and the beaches and islands of Auckland's fretwork coast.

New Zealand was also the last area on Earth to be settled by humans. It was less than 1000 years ago – just a blink of the eye in human history – that its islands were happened upon by voyaging Polynesians from the tropical region of the South Pacific. The first Europeans set foot in New Zealand only 230 years ago. But in that relatively brief period of habitation, the immigrants have drastically altered the land's natural patterns. The Maori fired South Island forests, tilled the lowlands and terraced headlands and hilltops. Then, from the 1870s onwards, European immigrants arrived in large numbers and set about transforming the land. They relentlessly felled the forests and planted pastures in their place. They built roads, railways and towns.

The towns have grown into cities, the roads into motorways, the harbours into great ports. Air travel has dramatically diminished the distances between New Zealand and the rest of the world. Isolation is no longer an economic or social constriction for New Zealanders. Paradoxically, modern communications with the rest of the world have led to the growth of nationhood and a stronger sense of New Zealand's unique cultural identity, derived as it is from a blend of its ancestral homelands, Polynesia and Europe. As more and more New Zealanders have travelled to what they call 'overseas', as they have observed and appreciated the ways the people of other nations live, so too has a sense of their own national consciousness developed.

They too have come into the clear light. This is the magic of New Zealand.

ABOVE   *Distance looks our way. International signpost at Cape Reinga.*

RIGHT   *Lighthouse at Cape Reinga, far north. Traditional departure point for Maori dead on their way to the spiritual homeland of Hawaiiki, Cape Reinga ('Place of Leaping' in Maori) is also the turbulent meeting place of the waters of the Tasman Sea and Pacific Ocean. The lighthouse is visible for 50 km (30 miles) out to sea.*

LEFT *Giant sand dune near Cape Reinga, in the far north of Northland.*

ABOVE *Driven inland by prevailing westerly winds, sand from the coast infiltrates the land near Cape Reinga.*

LEFT *Coastal living: houses cling to a hillside above Russell, Bay of Islands.*

ABOVE *Maori chief's dwelling, Rewa's Village, Kerikeri, Bay of Islands.*

OPPOSITE   *Russell township from Maiki Hill, Bay of Islands. Maiki Hill is the site of a flagstaff which once flew the Union Jack, symbol of British colonial authority in the early 1840s. The flagstaff was three times cut down by local Maori leader and rebel against the British military forces, Hone Heke, in 1844.*

ABOVE   *Once a notoriously rumbustious seaport, today Russell is the image of serenity. From the 1820s until the 1840s its sheltered bay made the town, then called Kororareka, a grogshop-filled haven for whalers and traders. Kororareka was sacked by Maori rebels in 1845.*

OPPOSITE *The sheltered bays, beaches and inlets of the Bay of Islands comprise Northland's most popular tourist playground.*

LEFT *The Hole in the Rock, Motukokaku Island, near Cape Brett, Northland, is navigable under suitable conditions.*

ABOVE *Ferry princess on her way to Russell.*

LEFT *Historic Maori Meeting House, Waitangi, and* (TOP) *a detail of the carvings.*

ABOVE *Treaty House, Waitangi. Here on February 6, 1840, the Treaty of Waitangi was signed by British Government representative, Governor William Hobson, and Maori leaders. The treaty ceded sovereignty of New Zealand to Queen Victoria, while supposedly protecting customary Maori rights to land and fisheries.*

PREVIOUS PAGE   *Central business district and skyline of Auckland, New Zealand's largest city, seen from the summit of the extinct volcanic cone of Mt Victoria in the North Shore suburb of Devonport.*

ABOVE   *Central Auckland from an observation deck of the Sky Tower, (328 m; 1076 ft).*

RIGHT   *One of Auckland's icons, the Harbour Bridge, with Bayswater Marina in the foreground.*

LEFT *The Viaduct Basin in central Auckland city, with its plethora of restaurants and bars, serves as a hub for Aucklanders and visitors alike.*

ABOVE *A dockside bar, Viaduct Basin.*

FOLLOWING PAGE, LEFT *Crowded moorings of pleasure craft at Westhaven Marina, Waitemata Harbour.*

FOLLOWING PAGE, RIGHT *Hauraki Gulf ferry and ferry building, central waterfront.*

NEXT FOLLOWING PAGE *Aucklanders gather on one of the oldest gun emplacements on North Head, Devonport. This was formerly a popular viewpoint for spectators of the Volvo Ocean Race and remains so for many harbour races.*

ABOVE *Tranquil anchorage on Waiheke Island, Hauraki Gulf, only 40 minutes by ferry from central Auckland.*

RIGHT *Sea-buffeted headlands at Piha, on Auckland's exposed west coast.*

LEFT *Cathedral Cove, Mercury Bay, Coromandel Peninsula.*

ABOVE *Lonely Bay, near Cook's Beach, where the English explorer and sea captain's first expedition to New Zealand observed the transit of the planet Mercury, November 9, 1769.*

FOLLOWING PAGE *Pauanui, a stylish holiday home subdivision on its own spit of land, viewed from Paku hill, Tairua, eastern Coromandel Peninsula.*

RIGHT   *Sunset over Oamaru Bay.*

FOLLOWING PAGE   *A tramper pauses above Emerald Lakes, Tongariro Crossing, in Tongariro National Park. The North Island's central plateau is a region of intense volcanic activity.*

RIGHT *Mt Ngauruhoe (2287 m; 7503 ft), New Zealand's most continuously active volcano, seen from the Desert Road, Tongariro National Park, central North Island. The Volcanic Plateau, occupying eastern Waikato and southern Bay of Plenty, contains many areas of active vulcanism.*

OPPOSITE *The steaming crater of Mt Ruapehu (2751 m; 9026 ft), the North Island's highest mountain and largest volcano. Ruapehu's slopes provide popular ski fields, but the skiing season was disrupted by the volcano's eruptions of 1995-96, the most spectacular since 1945.*

LEFT *The Waikato, the North Island's largest river, bisects the city of Hamilton, capital of the fertile Waikato region and fourth largest city in New Zealand.*

ABOVE *Novel souvenir shop, Tirau, Waikato.*

ABOVE *Stalactites and stalagmites, Aranui cave, Ruanuki Scenic Reserve, near Waitomo. The Waitomo caves are also famous for their glow-worms.*

RIGHT *Limestone formations in Aranui cave. These caves are channels which have been dissolved out of limestone by underground streams over thousands of years.*

PREVIOUS PAGE *A spectacular volcanic landform, Rainbow and Cascade terrace, dominates the landscape at Orakei Korako thermal area, near Taupo.*

RIGHT *Mount Maunganui's Ocean Beach on the Bay of Plenty coast attracts thousands of holiday-makers who come to enjoy the rolling surf and carnival atmosphere over the summer months. Mount Maunganui town is connected to the nearby city of Tauranga by a harbour bridge.*

ABOVE *A pioneer scene depicted on a mural, one of a series in the Bay of Plenty town of Katikati, which is the centre of a highly productive fruit-growing district.*

RIGHT *The blossom of the kiwifruit.*

OPPOSITE *A giant 'kiwifruit' publicises the region's best-known crop, near Te Puke, Bay of Plenty.*

LEFT *Pohutu geyser in full eruption, Whakarewarewa thermal area, Rotorua.*

ABOVE *The huge chasm of Mt Tarawera, near Rotorua, exposes ochre-coloured, volcanic earth. The ravine was created by a cataclysmic eruption in June, 1886, which covered the surrounding district in 2.5 m (8 ft) of mud and ash, engulfing the world-famous Pink and White Terraces and burying a neighbouring village, Te Wairoa. One-hundred-and-fifty-three people perished in the eruption.*

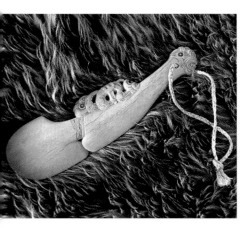

ABOVE *Carved Maori whalebone 'mere', or warclub.*

RIGHT *With their 'pois' (woven orbs) poised, children perform a traditional dance at a Maori cultural festival at Ruatahuna, Urewera region.*

LEFT *A young Maori warrior with headband and a felt pen 'moko' (facial tattoo), waiting to perform at a cultural festival at Ruatahuna.*

FOLLOWING PAGE *A plume of steam drifts from the crater of White Island, in the Bay of Plenty. An active volcano, the island was mined for sulphur deposits earlier this century until an eruption killed several miners. The proximity of the lower lip of the heated crater (right) to sea level makes the island a potential hazard for those living in Whakatane and Opotiki, closest coastal towns to the volcano.*

LEFT *The main street of Gisborne, largest town in Poverty Bay, the latter being so-named by Captain James Cook in 1769, in his frustration at being unable to obtain fresh food and water there for his expedition. Poverty Bay is in fact one of New Zealand's most fertile lowlands.*

ABOVE *Monument to James Cook (1728-1779), indefatigable explorer and leader of the first European expedition to land in New Zealand (October 9, 1769), on Kaiti Hill, Gisborne. In the background are the cliffs of Poverty Bay.*

ABOVE   *Yellowfin tuna and proud anglers, Gisborne Sport Fishing Club.*

RIGHT   *Eye of the Marlin, a prized deep sea game fish.*

OPPOSITE   *Catch-of-the-day. Taking home the tuna, Gisborne wharf.*

LEFT *Collecting shellfish from the ebbing tide, near Te Araroa, East Coast.*

ABOVE *The unique iridescence of New Zealand abalone shell, called 'paua', prized locally for inlays and jewellery making.*

LEFT *The view from Bluff Hill (102 m; 335 ft), Napier city, looking south over Hawke Bay towards Cape Kidnappers.*

ABOVE *Marine Parade and Art Deco building, Napier. After the city was devastated by an earthquake on February 3, 1931, Napier (population is estimated at 55,500) was rebuilt, largely in Art Deco architectural style, on land uplifted from the seabed by the earthquake.*

ABOVE *A gliding Australasian gannet (Morus serrator), known as 'takapu' by the Maori.*

RIGHT *Limestone cliffs at Cape Kidnappers, Hawke Bay, site of one of the few mainland gannet colonies in the world which is readily accessible to the public. There are about 6500 pairs of gannets in the breeding colony today.*

FOLLOWING PAGE *Mt Taranaki (2518 m; 8260 ft), a dormant volcanic cone, overlooks its region's ring plain. In the foreground is Lake Mangamahoe, near New Plymouth, the capital city of the Taranaki region.*

LEFT *Wellington city and harbour, from Mt Victoria.*

FOLLOWING PAGE LEFT *Bold design and construction have renewed the heart and waterfront of central Wellington in the 1990s. On the left is the Old Town Hall, on Civic Square.*

FOLLOWING PAGE RIGHT *Parliament buildings, Wellington. The House of Representatives (foreground) was completed in 1922. The 'Beehive' (background), which houses ministerial offices, the Prime Minister's Department and the Cabinet Room, was completed in 1981. Wellington has been the capital of New Zealand since 1865.*

ABOVE *The restored birthplace of New Zealand's best-known writer, Katherine Mansfield Beauchamp (1888-1924), allows visitors to glimpse family life in middle-class Victorian Wellington. The house in Tinakori Road, Thorndon, is administered by the Katherine Mansfield Birthplace Society.*

RIGHT *The sheltered inner city suburb of Oriental Bay provides majestic harbour views for its hillside residents.*

FOLLOWING PAGE *The Lady Norwood Rose Garden and surrounding Botanical Gardens crown the hills of Kelburn, above central Wellington.*

LEFT *Deceptively still waters below the lighthouse at Castlepoint, on the exposed and often-turbulent Wairarapa coast.*

ABOVE *Inter-island passenger and car ferry* Arahura *approaches Wellington harbour after its 3-hour journey across Cook Strait from Picton, in the Marlborough Sounds. Ferries run at regular intervals between the North and South Islands, day and night.*

LEFT *A mailboat on its delivery run to houses in the Marlborough Sounds, where sea transport still supersedes the automobile, and a jetty is more useful than a garage.*

ABOVE *Ferns, Abel Tasman National Park.*

ABOVE   *Sampling the vintages at Cairnbrae Winery, Blenheim, Marlborough.*

RIGHT   *High sunshine hours and alluvial soils make the Marlborough region New Zealand's premier white wine producing area. Pictured is Hunter Wines Bluff Vineyard, Awatere valley, near Blenheim.*

FOLLOWING PAGE LEFT   *Suntrap Restaurant, Kaikoura, in the shadow of the Kaikoura Range.*

FOLLOWING PAGE RIGHT   *Rural mailbox, Marlborough.*

ABOVE *Airborne beer can, Empire Hotel, West Coast.*

RIGHT *Provisions of yesteryear: shelves in a store in Shantytown,
a recreated colonial settlement near Greymouth.*

LEFT *Nikau Palms café and crafts shop at Punakaiki. Nikau palms reach 10 m (32 ft) in height and grow in lowland and coastal forests. Their flower spikes appear in summer, from December to February.*

ABOVE *Relentless westerlies and a wind-driven sea have sculpted the Pancake Rocks at Punakaiki.*

FOLLOWING PAGE *Lush native bush, Ship's Creek, West Coast.*

NEXT FOLLOWING PAGE *Canoeing at sunset on the Okarito Lagoon, Westland National Park.*

ABOVE *Café and neo-Gothic Arts Centre, formerly part of the University of Canterbury, Christchurch.*

RIGHT *A crumby existence. Café patrons, Arts Centre, Christchurch.*

OPPOSITE *Tram transport, reintroduced in 1995, takes tourists on a loop around central Christchurch. Pictured is Worcester Street, with Christchurch Cathedral in the background.*

LEFT *A screen of willows shelters punters on the River Avon, which meanders through central Christchurch.*

ABOVE *As English as the English? The dining Hall at Christ's College, boarding and day school for boys, in Christchurch. Founded in 1850 for sons of landed gentry, the school was based firmly on English public school principles.*

LEFT *A sea-drowned valley of an extinct volcano, Akaroa Harbour penetrates deeply into Banks Peninsula.*

ABOVE *The Mediterranean meets Canterbury – at French Farm Winery, Akaroa, Banks Peninsula. The Akaroa area was settled by immigrants from France in August, 1840, in the hope of making the South Island a French colony. When they arrived the British flag was already flying, however, the Treaty of Waitangi having been signed just six months earlier, making New Zealand a British colony. French influence endures nevertheless, in place-names in and around Akaroa.*

RIGHT *Grapes, a legacy of the French settlers.*

PREVIOUS PAGE *The Church of the Good Shepherd, in the Mackenzie Country, keeps a lonely watch over Lake Tekapo and the Southern Alps.*

LEFT *Foothills and mountains near Lake Tekapo.*

ABOVE *A braided river course, South Island high country.*

RIGHT *Fed by snowfields, the Tasman Glacier, at 29 km (18 miles) New Zealand's longest ice flow, makes its inexorable way down the eastern slopes of the Southern Alps.*

FOLLOWING PAGE *The roof of New Zealand. The country's highest peak, Mt Cook (3754 m; 12,316 ft, left) and neighbouring Mt Tasman surmount clouds in the Southern Alps. Mount Cook is also known by its Maori name, Aorangi ('cloud piercer').*

ABOVE   *Moeraki Boulders, embedded in the sands of Hampden Beach, North Otago.*

RIGHT   *The naturally spherical boulders of Moeraki are concretions formed by the accumulation of lime salts around a nucleus on the sea floor, about 60 million years ago. Early whalers called the beach Vulcan's Foundry, thinking it resembled the remains of a giant's game of bowls.*

LEFT *The architecture of Otago University, Dunedin, displays the solid confidence of the Victorian era. Founded in 1869, the university was the first in New Zealand.*

ABOVE *The ornate interior of Olveston House, Dunedin. The discovery of gold in Otago in 1861 fuelled early prosperity in nearby Dunedin, which during the 1860s became New Zealand's leading commercial centre.*

FOLLOWING PAGE *Frost on a farm at Macraes Flat, Central Otago. The cold winters and hot dry summers make Central Otago's climate the most extreme in New Zealand.*

ABOVE *Everybody lends a hand crutching (clipping wool from the hindquarters of a sheep) at Longslip Station, Lindis Pass.*

LEFT *Free at last! A 'flying' lamb at Loch Linnhe Station.*

RIGHT *Muster, Loch Linnhe Station, near Queenstown.*

OPPOSITE *TSS* Earnslaw *began service in 1912, serving run-holders who farmed around Lake Wakatipu. Today it takes visitors on the lake from its port of Queenstown (background).*

ABOVE *Bungy jumping above Queenstown. In the background is Lake Wakatipu and the Remarkables mountain range.*

LEFT *A Skyline Gondola viewed from Bob's Peak, above Queenstown.*

FOLLOWING PAGE *Sunrise makes pastel patterns on the waters of Glendhu Bay, on Lake Wanaka, Otago.*

NEXT FOLLOWING PAGE *Eerie stillness after rain on Milford Sound, Fiordland National Park, Southland. Mitre Peak looms darkly above the water (left).*

LEFT *End of the line, end of the mainland. Wharf at Bluff Harbour, Southland.*

ABOVE *MV* Milford Wanderer *and dolphins on remote Dusky Sound, Fiordland National Park.*

ABOVE *Faithful High Country trio: a farmer and his dogs driving sheep beside the road to Milford.*

RIGHT *Fields of wild flowers on the road to Milford.*

FOLLOWING PAGE *The sound of silence. The tranquil waters of Doubtful Sound, a several-branched fiord in Fiordland National Park.*